So
Many Reasons
Men Stay Single

By

Bret Eschmeyer

Strategic Book Group

Strategic Book Group
P.O. Box 333
Durham CT 06422

www.StrategicBookClub.com

ISBN: 978-1-60911-676-7

Table of Contents

Acknowledgements

With a book like this the list to thank is immense. First off, thank you to my inspiration, the hundreds of women who have turned me down or have just given me pieces that fit all too well in this book. Your quick judgments and inaccurate assumptions about me led to this amazing piece of work. My co-workers from several jobs with their water cooler talk also helped inspire me to make sure I got all of this in writing. Thank you to my co-workers from the University of Colorado that dared me to write all of these down. I know it's not the 23,641 or whatever number I finished calling off at the office, but it is more than enough to prove my original point back in 1999 when our banter started. Thank you to my close friends Patricia, Michelle, and Sean who were the first to read it and to give me a sense that it could be funny enough to sell and would make people laugh. If you don't like the book, blame them cause they must have the same sense of humor I do. To my sister-in-law Stephanie, who got a bit upset when I told her about the book and the premise of it. She pointed out that I shouldn't generalize, and I take that to heart every day. She is a wonderful person, and if I could find someone that could come close to her as a woman I would be a very lucky man, much like my brother Chad. To my parents, Ken and Judy, who weren't too keen on the idea of the book yet have set a wonderful example of what a marriage can and should be after over forty years together. To my friends Richard and Judy, thank you for all the moral support you have provided these past three and a half years with everything. To my great friends Alan and Dawn, you have seen me through more horrible dates than anyone, and I didn't even share 50 percent of them with you. But your blind faith that someone would come along all these years kept me trying, even though in the end we all came to the same conclusion. I cherish your friendship. I am blessed to have each of you listed above in my life.

To my agency, Writers Literary Agency, thank you for seeing the book for its potential and for putting me in touch with a great publisher. To my publishing company, Strategic Book Publishing, thank you for cleaning up this book and making it look great. Let's face it, I can be rough around the edges when it comes to writing. The end result is terrific. This has been a great experience in seeing my thoughts develop into something for the world to see. Without the help of every dedicated person there this dream would not have been possible.

Introduction

Let's be honest here, this book is not meant to be taken seriously. Most of the points are extremely true, I have lived or heard from others probably about 90 percent of them, but it still doesn't mean men want to be single. These are the reasons we end up staying single.

The problem is that people want instant gratification in life and that instant connection with someone new often referred to as "chemistry." Women want this chemistry to be off the charts but at the same time say they want a man to be a gentleman. Except what they really want is a bad boy they can convert to a gentleman so they know he will have a wild side. What women don't realize is that even the nice guy has a wild side; he's just very reserved with who he shows it to, how, and when.

I am a single male that in my mid 30's has never been in a serious relationship. Immediately red flags go up, and people ask, what is wrong with you? The answer is that I am still not sure. I own my own home as well two cars, including a midlife crisis car that I bought at age 33 – a 2004 Mustang GT Convertible black with tan top and tan interior (it sounds like a beast and is really fun to drive). I have investments that didn't get washed away in the Great Recession. I scuba dive; have season tickets to my local pro football team (yes it's the Denver Broncos); go to Rockies, Nuggets, and Avalanche games; love to get up to the mountains for drives, site seeing, hiking, etc. (although I've never skied). I am close with my family. I keep a few great friends that I would do anything for. I love animals. I'm big into travel and try to do one big dive trip a year and try to see my brother and his family at least once a year as well as spend weekends in the mountains (it helps that my parents have a nice house in a beautiful part of Colorado--I get room service and everything). Everyone that really knows me says I'm a really great guy.

The problem is my dates and other women don't see a wild side in me. They don't ask about anything from the past too much like my spur of the moment cross-country road trip (Massachusetts to California in a week would be considered that). Or about the time, while living in South Dakota, I went to a conference in Missouri for a weekend and got home Monday morning at 7 a.m. because we stopped at a baseball game in Kansas City, after taking a three hour detour to hit an Outlet Mall (trust me, for South Dakota boys that was a big deal at the time). We could also talk about petting sharks while diving or chasing a shark with my dive buddy my first day after certification and finding ourselves alone without a boat for at least ½ a mile when we surfaced and debating whether or not to swim to shore that was a good two miles away.

Also apparently guys are supposed to show confidence. It's hard to show confidence when you've never had a serious relationship by the time you get to my age. I know who I am, and I'm comfortable in whom I am, but apparently that's not enough. Here's my philosophy on it. I think even Thomas Edison a few times must have thought "What the hell?" when trying to invent the light bulb. I mean let's face it; it took him nearly 1,000 tries to get it right. So what kept him going? My guess is that at about every one hundredth attempt or so he found one that could actually last a few days, and he thought he'd gotten it right. But then it would burn out, and he'd still have hope that he would actually find the right filament. My predicament is much the same, except I haven't had enough tries that got far enough along to where I could say, "Hot damn I'm getting close, I can feel it."

All this circles back to one thing, and that's actually giving it a chance, whether it's a person, a date, a relationship, etc. One person can't just give it a chance though; it takes effort on both sides. Because we have become such a society of instant gratification, people can't stand to wait for the pot of gold at the end of the rainbow. So they pretend either that they can't see the end of the rainbow, or that they've found the end of the rainbow, and while the pot isn't filled with gold they'll try to make diamonds from the coal. In either case people get hurt, in one because someone wasn't given a chance, in the other because someone hoped for something that wasn't there.

In the end this is just a humorous take on male and female relationships and on social stigmas placed on men and women. It is not to be taken seriously. It is to be laughed at and enjoyed. It could be considered politically incorrect though it's probably closer to socially incorrect. Several people have seen parts or all of this work, and they have come away laughing and saying how they know so many people who resemble these comments. If you do not have a sense of humor, please don't read this. I don't want you to be offended.

Let me also say this, by no means is this book meant to categorize or generalize men and women, although I'm sure it will be read as such. Each person is completely unique in their own way, sometimes good and sometimes not so good, but either way we are all unique. That is what makes the process of dating and getting to know what each of us is and is not compatible with so intriguing.

For a final note, if you are a single female, mid-twenties to mid-thirties, with stunning good looks, and are financially able to take care of me, I'm still on the lookout, just come find me. For a list of women I would make myself available for, I may put up a list on my author's web page, just take a look.

Chapter 1

Courting

Flowers are a must, even if you're allergic.

You can't eat the chocolates before you give them to her.

You have to keep your Viagra stash hidden; women always search through your medicine cabinet to see what you have.

You can't fart around her for the first six months, minimum.

You can't belch around her for at least four months, unless it's a little polite one. I'd advise you not to risk it though.

Scratching is inappropriate until after you have sex, otherwise she might think you are just with her cause you're horny.

You can't slurp spaghetti at a restaurant or at home with her.

You can't slurp soup at a restaurant or at home with her.

The Playboys can't be left out on the coffee table, just in case she decides to drop by.

If you are getting serious, she has to meet your parents within three weeks of becoming exclusive, no matter how badly your parents will embarrass you.

Courting is simply a painful experience, like getting an enema twice a week.

Take it from personal experience. On several occasions, I have started getting to know and like a woman over the course of two, three, or four months. In each

2

case, she said she wasn't ready to date me but wanted to continue to get to know me. Finally, I found the reason why. She had been seeing someone else the whole time, or even just part of the time, and had decided to see the "other guy" only. A couple of the girls had fallen in love; a couple of the girls had even gotten engaged. So much for being a nice guy, what a load of crap!

She expects you to open the door for her all the time, even if it's her front door and it's locked.

You have to do things she likes, even if you don't like them, just to show you care, like going to the opera. Oh, Barf!

You have to tell her that outfit is stunning on her, even if she looks like a hot air balloon in it.

You have to enjoy her cooking, even if she burned the salad!

You can't see her in a bathing suit for at least a month. Those are her rules.

You can't pick your nose in front of her, even if the booger is huge and plugging up your breathing.

You can never ask if she is ready for sex, cause that would mean you are too eager to get her in bed.

You must be able to tell if she wants to kiss you or not for the first time. If you make the move at the wrong time, it's over.

You shouldn't get gropy at all, until she starts to touch you, otherwise she'll think you are just with her for sex.

If you decide to go to an art show, make sure it's not one of those "erotic" art shows, unless you've already had sex, and she's into that kind of thing, otherwise she'll think you are just with her for the sex.

Courting is different from dating. I just don't know how, neither does any other man, and no woman will ever be willing to explain it to us.

From what I understand, courting is much more intense. Guys don't like intense, so be careful.

Somehow in courting, you must be able to have fun,

be serious, and have a plan in your life, while being able to maintain spontaneity. Good luck with that requirement.

If she asks you in on the first date, be very careful until you find out if she has roommates or not. They could be in the hallway acting as spies.

When you first meet her pets, be extremely careful not to piss them off. If you do, her pets will never like you, and you will soon be banished from her pants and from her life.

When first meeting her friends, be very careful that you do not spend too much time talking to any of them. You have to continue to give her tons of attention, otherwise her friends will not like you and think you are with her for the sex.

Even though men date women for sex, that reason has to be concealed until much later on in the relationship, like the wedding night.

When first meeting her parents, you have to check many times to ensure that your fly is zipped up all the way. This serves many purposes, including not having an embarrassing moment or not having them think you are just a horny guy wanting to make it with their daughter.

Most likely, the first time you meet her parents will be for a dinner. Remember eating rules, such as not slurping your spaghetti or drinking the soup directly from the bowl. Parents, for some reason, don't appreciate some guy after their daughter if he has table manners that they don't approve of.

Watch Out! Chick flicks, here you come.

You can't let her catch you in your grunderwear (gross underwear, every guy has at least four pair) until well after you've seen her in a bathing suit for the first time. Although this could be a great test to see if she'd stick around or bail.

You can never let her see you sweat on the first, second, or even third date, unless of course you have incorporated a physical activity into the date.

If she happens to come over to your place, you have to make sure you clean up ALL your clothes in your bedroom, just in case she's snoopy, and especially if you leave your grunderwear on the lamp on a regular basis.

You have to make sure you have the soda she likes at your place just so you don't make her mad.

Don't tick her off in any way, shape, or form. Remember the saying, "There is no fury like a woman scorned."

No matter how hard you try, you will screw up something. Especially since you are not allowed to know what a woman thinks or feels about anything.

At some point in time, she will want you to cook for her. Unfortunately, Hungry Man TV dinners don't count.

Carryout or delivery doesn't count when she wants you to fix dinner for her either.

First dates are always difficult.

It is still expected that the man pays for the first date, even with equal rights running amuck.

First dating can be expensive, especially if you are dating a lot. Let's take a quick look. Dinner in a decent restaurant is about $20 per meal, plus drinks $5/each, dessert $5/each, and tip. Grand total is approximately $60, give or take a few dollars.

Do this five times in a month and spend $300. Or you could get two great tickets to a football game or basketball game, possibly both, with a buddy for a lot less hassle.

Do this for an entire year and spend $3,600. Or you could get season basketball and football tickets, take a trip to Hawaii, have a great time in Las Vegas, put a down payment on a new car, by a big screen TV for the living room, buy a jet ski, … take your pick on the possibilities.

We haven't even discussed going to movies, or bowling, or mini golf, or going for drinks, which would be a typical second event for a first date.

Going to the movies now can cost between $7 and $8 per ticket. Being the gentleman you are, of course you pay on the first date. Now include a couple of drinks $6/each, and some candy, $5, and you are set for event number two, total about $30-$35. So for one evening, dinner and movies will cost you about $90-$100.

Bowling can actually be rather expensive for two people as well. Let's look. Say you only bowl two games. At $2-$3/game per person, with shoe rental of $1 each, and $3/drink while you are bowling for each of you, your total is about $25. One evening of dinner and bowling will cost you around $85.

Just going for drinks could be the most expensive,

especially if you sit and talk for several hours. Each drink at a club, tavern, or saloon will probably cost in the neighborhood of $4-$5. So if you each have three drinks and talk for three hours, your total for this second event will be about $30. Again, the combined evening would cost about $90.

So if you add in a second activity to the first date, and have five new first dates in a month, you could spend around $500 in one month. That's just downright scary.

Doing that for the course of an entire year would cost almost $6,000. For that amount, go back to school and pick up college chicks that think Taco Bell is grand cuisine. Plus you could get a second degree to top it off as an added bonus.

Why is it okay for a woman to play mind games but not a man?

If a woman want to find someone to be with, why do they "play" hard to get?

Chasing a woman who is playing hard to get is more frustrating than going fishing and finding out your fishing pole is broken.

Just so you know if you are not serious about her you can't take her to Vegas, ever. Think about it, Vegas, free alcohol, and cheap wedding chapels.

Of course in these days we must talk internet dating. That's a scary proposition itself.

First off, never trust a woman who's only picture online is a Glamour Shot. It's like expecting the burger you get from a fast food restaurant to look like the commercials. It just won't happen.

Any time a woman uses the phrase "curvy" to describe her body type, she's very heavy and just doesn't want to accept that she's fat. You have been warned.

Other things to beware of are when she lists her hobbies as the theater and the arts. This does not mean movies. This means opera and plays, also known as the boredom zone for men.

Any woman that lists politics as an interest means she likes to argue and debate anything possible. This means fights will ensue, and you will miss out on sex for long periods of time and will sleep on the couch a lot.

If a woman lists long hair and tattoos as turn-ons, she is looking for a bad boy she can try to reform. This is the worst type of woman to meet as she is looking to mold a man into the type of person she wants in the end.

No woman truly wants a bad boy. In the end she wants a good person she can have a relationship with. It's just the idea of being with a bad boy she likes. So if there are signs she wants a bad boy, watch out, she is not ready for a real relationship yet.

Chapter 2

Activities as a Couple

You have to go hang out with her obnoxious friends and play bridge for evenings at a time. Forget about getting your couple friends together for poker night. Here's an idea, try couples Strip Poker night! Ha, yeah right, good luck with that one.

Dinner with a new couple just to make them feel good about being a couple. Even though he is a booger-picking moron, and she can't put her dress on forwards, ever, you still have to get together for a weekly dinner with them.

Unfortunately, vacations together have now become the norm. Why do I say unfortunately? You must visit her parents and her relatives. If confused, refer to Chapter 6 for this one.

You go on a vacation to visit her long lost friend from kindergarten. Come to find out her friend is a 400 lb water balloon now who recently had to have the doorways widened in her house for her size. Her friend's husband is a 110 lb, 5'10" stick figure, who, aside from driving to work, has never seen the light of day. They don't clean their house, ever, and there is garbage and food all over, even in the guest bed. Wonder how that got there? Must be from the all-night sex session they had three weeks ago where he fed her the refrigerator for an hour and a half. Good luck getting any sleep there for the next week of your stay, or doing anything at all for that matter, except being grossed out constantly.

The vacations to Hawaii are now off. She doesn't want you having any chance to see another bikini. You can't go skiing in the mountains either, too many snow bunnies. The only options left are to visit relatives, hers and yours. AAAAGGGGGGHHHHH!!!!!

Remember that chick flick you saw the previews for? You are going to that tonight.

The problem with chick flicks is that they come out weekly. Why is this? Because with every chick flick, every female with a man in her life will mean two people going to see it. This is a very lucrative business for the Hollywood types, so they continue to roll out the crap. And it's not like when two women go to see it--they both want to be there. Hollywood is counting on women across the country dragging men to these movies kicking and screaming. It's extra revenue for them that the action movies don't get. Why don't action movies get this extra revenue? Because if a woman doesn't want to go, she won't go, no matter how much the man in her life asks her to see it with him. A woman should be honored that a guy wants to see a big explosion flick with her, but instead they just think it's disgusting, turn their nose up at it, and make you sleep on the couch just for asking her to go.

Bowling is a great couple's activity. So if you have never bowled before, get practicing. It is going to take a long time to get used to it. In other words, get prepared well in advance of ever dating anyone, unless you don't mind looking like a total dork.

Shooting pool is another great activity, but if you sucked at geometry this will be a tough game to figure out. Letting her win should be easy in this case. Just hope she isn't a poor sport and rubs it in your face all night.

For some reason it is expected that any activity you want to do she will join you in doing, such as visiting the car and truck show, attending the pro wrestling event at the arena, or watching an action movie. She hates all these things but will go with you just to ruin your good time with her misery.

You have to go to the opera because she wants to go and doesn't want to take a girlfriend. She has several female friends that would go; she just wants to see how much you squirm during the show.

You have to go to the ballet. It's even worse than the opera, but, again, it's a squirm test.

You have to go to the opening of an art gallery for the new wave artists, something you don't understand, but she wants to go and drags you with her.

You have to watch figure skating at the arena and act like it's an actual sport.

Going to pick out a new car just doesn't have the same appeal, especially after she says, "I want that car because it's a pretty color."

Going to pick out sheets and a comforter for the bed really bites. You just know she will get what she wants anyway and it's going to be flowery and foofy. So why do you have to go through fifty stores telling her you like this and this and this when she will get the ugliest one on the planet, typically with pink flowers?

You go to pick out furniture and see the black leather sofa you've been wanting for years. Instead, you get a nice sofa with a huge floral print because "it is more practical." Practical for what? Attracting bees?

Dinner as a couple can be an event for sure. McDonald's is not allowed because it's "too fattening." However, go out to a nice seafood dinner and she will get the lobster with extra butter and the baked potato with extra sour cream and butter. Yeah, that's a nice compromise. Not for your wallet, that's for sure.

When going to rent a movie, be prepared for something super sappy, such as "Sleepless in Seattle" or "Beaches" or that "Traveling Pants" one.

When renting a movie, these are not options because of the violence: "Hamburger Hill," "Platoon," the "Die Hard" series, or the "Rambo" series. Just to name a few.

Once you are a couple, sex drops from a potentially daily activity to a weekly or monthly activity. If you are lucky you may get it once a week, otherwise it's once a month, kind of like her PMS.

Once you have moved to couples stage, sex for her is no longer a fun activity but a chore. And she will always complain about having to do that chore, each and every month she has to do it.

You get to go pick out drapes for your new home. Why do you need to go? It's torture, you don't care, and she picks anyway.

You must help her pick out household accessories. What are household accessories? Does any guy know or care? No, this is just another way to torture you. Besides, who cares if the can opener's handle is black or white anyway? It's just a can opener!!

I suggest you learn how to play bridge or canasta. She will make sure to drag you to bridge or canasta-playing parties. For all guys that don't know, bridge and canasta are card games. At least I think they are. That's the rumor on the streets anyway.

Camping out can be fun, assuming you can get her into a two-person sleeping bag. If you can't find one, try taking two and zipping them together. If you can't accomplish this, then there is really no point in going camping.

Fishing requires a lot of effort on your part. There is

a very good chance she will get squeamish and not bait her own hook and will squeal each time you hook her worm, not your worm, just hers. The squealing alone will scare all the fish away.

Hunting … forget it.

Hiking might work, unless she doesn't like being physically active. Some women like being inside and reading trashy romance novels instead of being in the great outdoors.

Boating could work, just don't expect to take any female friends with you, especially if they wear bikinis and look good in them.

Mini golf is a good date activity, but for some reason it loses its luster after you've been a couple for awhile.

You have to spend time with her ugly, dull, boring friends and act like they are the greatest people on the planet.

Pretty soon ordering pizza and staying in is all you do. Actually that can be a plus, but you won't be able to show her off then.

After a while a hot date is when the pizza is fresh out of the oven and still 200 degrees.

Working out at the gym together, while bringing you closer together, could make her suspicious that you just want to watch the women's aerobics classes.

Going to the beach on the weekend can be fun. Most likely she will think you just want to go to check out all the women in their bikinis.

You should never go play paintball with her if she intends to be on the other team. She will be relentless in the pursuit of pounding you with paintballs, and you will acquire welts all over your body.

Learning karate or other martial arts forms together is not an option. She will most likely use it against you sometime down the road. Wearing a cup at all times would then become necessary if there was a strain in the relationship.

Learning pottery could be fun. If you are uncertain about that, just watch the movie "Ghost" or have her describe the movie to you. Trust me, it's a chick flick, she's already watched it a hundred times.

If you made a mess doing the pottery, you will be expected to clean everything up before it dries and gets really messy, and that can be a very fun activity to share together. Assuming she got muddy at all with the clay. Although she may be the type that doesn't like getting messy at all, so where is the fun in that?

You know things are really bad when you start doing the crossword and Sudoku puzzles in the newspaper together every day.

Going and picking out pets is a great thing to do. The only problem is if you break up she will take the dog, and you will get the cat that claws everything to bits, so you can't get that leather couch you've been wanting so much.

One activity that will end up happening sooner or later is her picking out your clothes and telling you what to wear to work, at home, when you go out together, even to bed, etc. This is one activity men need to avoid at all costs.

Going to the zoo always seems to be a good date activity, but once you become a couple there are only so many times you can see the same animals in the same cages being completely inactive all the time.

Ice-skating and roller skating are always possible date ideas. But after she finds out how clumsy you are at those things it could be the end of anything remotely good. She will think you have no coordination anywhere, including the bedroom, and that is definitely a very bad thing.

If you know how to dance this is a premium activity to do as pretty much every woman on the planet enjoys dancing. If, however, you are one of the millions of uncoordinated men in the world that have no rhythmic ability, like me, dancing is horrible. Women relate your ability to dance to your ability to move in the bedroom. Example: bad dancer = bad in bed. It's not necessarily true, but that's how a woman computes it.

There are several types of dancing you can try, but ballroom, salsa, or some of the other more formal ones you could learn. However, she may take this as a sign you are trying to hit on the other women in the class. This would mean more sleeping time on the couch.

Unfortunately once you become a couple, cleaning the house becomes one of the really exciting activities you do together frequently. Typically at least once a week, or in other words, more often than you have sex.

As cleaning becomes a typical activity for you and your significant other, you get to clean all the toilets and get assigned all the other of the grossest jobs too.

Cleaning gutters is something you are no longer allowed to hire the neighbor's kid to do. When it comes time to clean the outside of the house, you have to do that yourself.

Landscaping is something else that becomes a couple activity. While it can be fun, you get to do all the backbreaking work, like moving all the rocks twenty times over since she doesn't like how they are arranged or doing all the pavers in the 101 degree summer heat.

Unfortunately doing laundry together becomes an activity you do as a couple also. And no matter what you do, you will never, ever, fold the sheets the way she likes them.

Doing the dishes is another thing you "get" to do as a couple. Of course you will never put them in the dishwasher the way she likes them. Nor will you get each pot scrubbed enough to her liking.

Why isn't making breakfast together naked an activity couples can enjoy? Wouldn't it make the entire meal more interesting?

On that note, why isn't making any meal together naked an activity couples could enjoy? I would think it definitely could make the dessert more interesting, if things even get to that point. Or you could take dessert to the bedroom. Too bad women don't like that idea.

Chapter 3

Moving In Together

She will insist, at some point in time, that when you run errands you pick up some feminine products for her.

It will always happen that when picking up her feminine products the cashier will ask for a price check on those products.

Women must have flower sheets on the master bed.

They must make the bedroom look and feel foofy.

Women hang up gaudy junk on the walls called "wall hangings" and say they are decorations, while your beer babe posters and neon lights are not welcome and too loud and obnoxious to stay.

Women think socks and underwear must be neatly folded.

You must leave the toilet seat down for them so they don't fall in. Here's an idea for them, "Look before you squat!!"

They don't put the toilet seat up for you.

Women feel a need to vacuum weekly, not only whenever company is coming over.

Women feel a need to dust weekly. Why dust? It just makes you have to vacuum.

Women want the garbage taken out all the time. No more pizza box furniture for you. Damn!

Recycling is always a must for women. Even if the service is not provided by your garbage removal company, you must now provide that service for the house and drive thirty miles each way to the recycling center.

No matter how much you try to explain it to them,

women will never understand men's obsessions with power tools. Tim Allen tried mightily for years on "Home Improvement" to enlighten his wife but to no avail. Don't waste your time as he did his; it's a pointless effort.

You are no longer allowed to watch sports 24/7. Oh, man, how will you keep up with current events?

Women think soap operas are real-life and realistic. In other words, everyone is sleeping with three people and has gorgeous kids and is financially loaded. So much for your dream of working at McDonald's for free food.

Women don't understand scratching and adjusting. This makes it harder to do the needed things once you live together. You must run and hide every time it's necessary to scratch or adjust. Ten times a day at least for most men, luckily pets don't care.

Under no circumstances will you be allowed to do the laundry your way.

Under no circumstances will you be allowed to do the dishes your way.

Women always need to talk when you have the game on. Of course, since you can find a game on just about 24/7, this can be a good way to avoid talking all together. Break out the corn nuts and beef jerky, baby, alright!

Poker night at your house now consists of vegetable plates and women complaining of cramping, rather than cigars, beer, and chips and dip.

Men's night out involves a half hour discussion, meaning you continually promise the whole time that you will not talk to any woman and that the only thing you will do is talk to your friends, be the designated driver, and avoid looking at other women.

Now that you are living together, sex isn't as exciting, especially after you've seen some of the things she does during "her time of the month."

Now that you are living together, sex isn't as exciting because you can't get caught by one of your roommates, or one of her roommates depending on whose place you are at, on the living room couch or in the kitchen or in the bathroom.

Dinner out still doesn't mean at a fast food restaurant.

Often times, she still expects to be wined and dined before you get to have sex.

Moving in together doesn't necessarily mean more frequent box springs tests.

You can't drink the milk out of the carton any more because it's more likely you'll get caught.

You are very lucky if you can continue to keep your car and hunting magazines in the bathroom. The Playboys must go.

The pool table in the den is not a place for sex any more. The pool table has been replaced by a sewing machine.

Losing the pool table means you can't watch sports anymore. Once you give up one hobby, you end up losing them all. Instead, she watches her soaps on your big screen TV.

The living room can't have a TV in it any more because that is now where people gather and have "meaningful" conversations.

You can't have the guys over to play video games on your PlayStation.

She makes you get rid of the PlayStation.

You can no longer keep your copy of the Pamela and Tommy Lee sex tape.

Your DVD player and monster stereo system now has to play chick flicks such as "Fried Green Tomatoes" and "Beaches," rather than the sound-busting "Top Gun" and "Mission Impossible" that the system was meant to digitally enhance and make better and clearer.

Your rebuilt 1964 Camaro has to sit outside of the one car garage for her 1990 station wagon (any make).

You now have to drive the station wagon most of the time to pick up all the materials for the baby's new room as you build it.

Snacking after meals is considered rude, even if you finished everything and are still hungry.

Belching at the dinner table is not considered polite and doesn't say, "Damn that was a good meal" to her.

After three helpings, you aren't allowed to take the rest and sit in front of the TV.

Dessert is not supposed to be eaten first and definitely not within the first ten seconds of sitting down.

You actually have to eat at the dining room table. You didn't even know you had a dining room table. You figured it was just a place to store papers and the mail.

You must eat where food is allowed, and the couch is not one of those places.

She doesn't allow food to leave the kitchen, so adding whip cream to the sex life must be done in the kitchen too, I guess.

You can never ask what she uses her feminine products for. Of course, why the hell would you want to know anyway?

Showering must be done individually, in other words, you can't join her any more after you are married, only when you are still dating.

You can never be in the bathroom getting ready for bed if she has to use the toilet.

She can use your razor on her legs; you can't use her razor for your face. Though why would you want to do that?

After you are married, you aren't allowed to shave her legs any more because she doesn't feel it's erotic like it used to be.

If you miss the toilet when aiming, you must clean it up right away. It can't wait till the monthly floor cleaning like it used to.

The kitchen and bathrooms must be cleaned more than once every two months; you get to clean it every other week, she gets the weeks in between. In other words, now it's clean every week and you are doing it twice a month instead of once every two months.

The constant fumes from the regular cleaning of the kitchen and bathrooms make you dizzy and nauseas a lot.

You now have a house and have to take care of the yard, instead of living in a condo where you don't have a yard to worry about.

Having a yard now means you have to mow the lawn weekly, bag the clippings, and dispose of them appropriately.

You must also keep the shrubs trim. Why do you need shrubs? Who the hell ever thought of the word "shrub"?

You have to buy tons of lawn tools now that you never thought you'd ever have because she's moved you to a house.

Since you wanted the dog, you get to clean up the dog poop, even though she now thinks it's her dog.

Every man needs his own room in the house he can call his own, for an office, library, pool table, entertainment center, game room, etc. Under no circumstances should the woman ever be allowed to decorate this room in any way. This is the one room where beer lights and football posters are allowed. If any man actually gets to have this, please let me know. It would be a first in the history of society, and I want to visit.

Chapter 4

Clothes

Ripped jeans are no longer appropriate attire for you.

Ripped underwear is no longer appropriate attire for you. This one really sucks.

She now can wear baggy sweats around the house constantly, not allowing you to get turned on by her figure at all.

The sweats you have lounged around in since freshman year in college get thrown out and burned without your knowledge.

You are now forced to get dressed up in a tuxedo when you go out to her new favorite activity, THE OPERA!

You must look nice to meet the friends that she made yesterday when grocery shopping.

The baseball hat you've had since your college days (three years ago) has got to go because it's just too dumpy.

While it takes you two minutes to decide what to wear, don't plan on going anywhere with her for at least an hour as she stares into the closet trying to determine what outfit is most appropriate for the occasion. Whatever you do, don't get into the "Does this look good on me?" trap. Leave the room, leave the house even, go outside, and do some yard work so you can't get bit in the ass with that question.

If you ever get asked the question "Does this make me look fat?" your answer can't just be "No." Even though you are thinking "It's not the outfit that makes you look fat, it's your fat," under no circumstances should this EVER exit your mouth. Your answer must be, at the absolute minimum, "Hell no girl, you are stunning in that outfit!" Anything less and you will be stuck there for the next thirty minutes as she tries on ten outfits trying to find the right one. Never fall into that trap.

Never fall into the "Does this make my butt look big?" trap either. Of course the first thought to cross your mind is, "That doesn't make your butt look big, your ass is really huge," under no circumstances can you say this out loud if you ever want to live. If this question comes up, refer back to the answer above.

Never fall into the "Does this outfit make me look too short?" trap. Again, revert back to the answer above. Under no circumstances should your thought of "Hell girl, I've seen pigmies taller then you," ever be spoken out loud.

Never fall into the "Does this outfit make me look too tall?" trap. Once again you must revert back to the answer above. You should never say what you are thinking with this one either, which would commonly be "Hey, since you can look over the refrigerators, can you see what the score of the game is in the electronic section for me?"

Never fall into the "Is this outfit too old?" trap. Use the answer above again for this one. If you don't, not only will you be stuck looking at ten more outfits right then, but you will also go shopping with her for clothes and will spend an entire day in the mall looking at outfits, until she can find at least five outfits to replace that old one. Never say what you are thinking to this which is often, "The outfit isn't old, it's the body it's drooping off of that's wearing down."

Never fall into the "Is this outfit too bright?" trap. Revert back above once again for the answer to this question. Don't ever say what you are thinking to this question either, such as "Well we both know the person wearing that outfit isn't bright" or "I think you just alerted the ships at sea to all turn left that thing is so bright."

38

Never fall into the "Is this outfit too dull?" trap. Your answer for this is above as well. Do not say what you are thinking here either, something like "It does match your mom's personality well."

Women need a pair of shoes for every outfit, no questions are allowed to be asked about the logic behind this either.

Women can't have this pair of shorts or pants go with those two or three shirts, instead there is a separate pair of shorts or pants with every top. No top can be used for two different bottoms either. Their logic is that no two shades are exactly alike. However, blue jeans are blue jeans damn it and can work with just about anything.

Men only need four or five pairs of shoes, max. Tennis shoes for casual wear, dress shoes for work and weddings (anything else formal falls in this category also), sandals for the pool or the beach, and hiking boots for working in the yard and hiking or other hard physical activities in the wilderness. And a pair of basketball shoes as well, if they have bad ankles and play basketball a lot.

Men realize that jeans can be worn with all kinds of tops, so four or five good pairs of jeans are all that is needed. This is because we wear dress clothes to work, and we come home and change, but the jeans don't get worn more than a few hours, and unless something is spilled on them, they are good to wear for several days, women just can't stand or understand this concept.

Women have fifty pairs of jeans, because they think they need every shade imaginable. To a woman, blue isn't just blue, it's indigo, navy, royal, teal, turquoise, ocean, sky, light, dark, aqua, midnight, and any other label you can slap on a color. Make one up and tomorrow it's a bestseller to women.

The shading of jeans doesn't just go for jeans either. It goes for socks, shirts, blouses, sweaters, underwear, nail polish, lipstick, hair coloring, eye shadow, belts, earrings, necklaces, etc., you name it. Absolutely amazing, but you can see why there's 500 women's fashion magazines on the market, just to try and color all this crap.

How many closets are in the house? Because they will all get filled with her seasonal clothes. She will have to rotate clothes between closets for the different seasons. Except for you, you get a small corner in the bedroom closet, and that's all you get for the rest of your life.

You will never pick out your own clothes to buy ever again.

Be prepared to get the ugliest sweater you've ever seen. This will happen several Christmases.

Be prepared to get the ugliest ties you have ever seen on many occasions at Christmas as well.

Don't be surprised if you receive ugly ties and sweaters on your birthday too.

You'd better get her the perfect outfit for Christmas. She won't hesitate to tell you directly that it sucks. And then she'll go and exchange it.

If you hate the sweater you get, you still have to tell her it's perfect, even if it's the worst thing ever designed to be worn by man.

Shopping seems to be a national pastime for women. Unfortunately clothing is the most common purchased item. Clothing for them, not you.

If you have an unfinished basement it may be wise to finish it off into one massive closet for her to store her loot from constantly shopping.

You were only allowed to help her pick out lingerie before you were living together, now she doesn't like to buy lingerie or look sexy for you at all.

You must be prepared to try and turn her on at some point in time in a really tight pair of bikini underwear that she likes, which is two sizes too small and cuts off circulation to certain vital body parts.

Even if you've never worn a suit in your life, she will make you have a suit for the one time a year you go to a fancy restaurant with her.

In that case, watch out for the potential of the ugly tie syndrome.

Be prepared to get ties from your kids as Christmas gifts that are supposed to go with that suit.

Unfortunately there is a very good chance after you've been married awhile that you could get underwear as a Christmas gift.

If underwear is not the gift of choice, socks will be.

If you are lucky enough to not get socks or underwear

for Christmas, the ugly tie is next in line for you.

One thing going for you at least is overalls are out of style. If you work outside in the yard much though there is a chance she will find the last pair on earth for you to wear while working outside.

After she has kids, all her desire to look and dress sexy will go out the window.

Of course her favorite "designer" is unleashing a new line of clothes, and she just must get all of it.

Her other favorite designer has all new seasonal lines for year-round. Be ready for her to revamp her entire wardrobe yet not get rid of anything. This means you must look for a way to expand closet space.

Be careful of one very important thing, her belt collection. The 300 belts can be used as weapons at any time.

Maybe you should be careful of another very important thing as well and that is her stiletto heel collection. Stomping, kicking, throwing, stabbing, etc., can all be examples of extraneous uses for stiletto heels. There may be times wearing a cup is appropriate.

Only if you are extremely lucky will you ever see her in her cheerleading outfit from college.

There is one time when her being a biker chick would be a good thing and that is when you want her to wear biker chaps and nothing else for a night of fun. Of course if she has gotten out of shape, wearing chaps would be a very bad thing.

Why is it you can't get her to have a collection of lingerie from Victoria's Secret like she has of granny panties?

Why is it that once you get married she stops wearing those skin tight pants that you loved so much the first year you were together?

Don't you think there should be a weight limit on spandex? Oof.

There should probably be a weight limit on bikinis too, especially when you can't even tell when a woman has one on at the beach. Ugh.

G-strings and thongs should also have a weight limit. They can become completely obscured and you could lose your eyesight for life, should you ever happen upon this situation.

Midriff or belly shirts are other items that should also fall in the weight limit category.

Tight skirts went out of style for her on your evenings out the minute you became a couple, meaning there are no more secrets for you to guess at as now she is only wearing baggy pants....

What is the point of runway models wearing low cut blouses in the front when they are still built like eight-year-old boys? That's just not attractive at all.

Chapter 5

Wedding Planning
and the
Wedding Day

Why is it her day? Aren't you both involved?

You have to pick out a tuxedo.

The tuxedo has a cumberbund, known as a girdle in women's apparel.

You must help pick out flowers, as if you care what color of flower adorns the tables that you won't ever be sitting at to enjoy.

You must help to choose the kind of invitation to send out.

Your idea of an invitation will not, under any circumstances, work anyway. You know, the one that reads, "Hey yo, we're tyin' the knot, so show up at this location, this day, and this time, bring a present, open bar at the dance afterward."

You have to invite people you don't know. Either it's her wish, her parents' wish, or your parents' wish, no matter what.

Your wish doesn't matter, especially when wanting your friends to be there.

Sorry but you can't go to Vegas and hit the Elvis Love Chapel, it has to be something "classy."

The local bar is not an option for the dance afterward either.

You have to spend hours upon hours going to jewelry shops to find wedding bands. They must match and are way too expensive for something that won't fit in three years anyway because now that she landed you she will let herself go.

It finally dawns on you when ordering the cake that you have to share it with people you don't know. Here's a thought, get five of the eight layers as flavors you would never eat, keep the best three for yourself and for fun your wedding night (wink, wink). That way, you won't feel so guilty about giving the gross five layers away, especially since it's people you don't know and will never see again in your entire life.

You have to decide where to register for gifts, and no, Spencer Gifts doesn't count! Damn it, anyway.

The sporting goods sections of Target, Walmart, and Kmart are not allowed either for gifts.

Flowers and scented candles all over are a must for her, even if you are allergic.

She gets a shower and bachelorette party, you only get the bachelor party, and she won't allow anything other than alcohol at your party (i.e., no women). Meanwhile, she has five male strippers at her bachelorette party.

You have to pick out a church, even though church conflicts with Sunday football in the fall. You haven't been to a church since you were old enough to realize the schedule conflict.

The individual performing the ceremony, whether it is a rabbi, priest, minister, etc., has to sit you down to talk about the sanctity of marriage, even though around 60 percent of all marriages in the US end in divorce. A lot of good this three-hour session does here in the states. Wouldn't you rather be watching a baseball game, or even golfing or fishing?

You have to send everyone directions to the ceremony, reception, and dance. Make it all in one location and it's not that bad. The problem is, tradition still expects this, but everyone should know how to use MapQuest, or other mapping software packages, or online programs by now. Save the effort, just give them the locations and a good website for directions.

You now not only have to find a photographer to take pictures but a video company to tape the whole thing.

Most likely, you are paying for both the photographer and video company. Ahh, the wonderful expense (I mean experience) of getting married.

A wedding with a Hawaiian motif isn't acceptable, unless you are in Hawaii.

What's the chance you can afford to get married in Hawaii?

No sports themes are allowed either, like doing a tailgate party before the ceremony. Darn, I was looking forward to smoked sausages and brats.

Doing an informal picnic, like "Bring your own food" doesn't fly either. So be prepared to shell out a ton of money for the food for your 500 guests.

Remember, she wants to have a big, formal wedding, with all the trimmings.

If you have graduated college and have been on your own for awhile, don't expect any help from either set of parents in paying for this deal.

Don't expect her to help pay either. It's supposed to be the guy's responsibility to financially support the family, and that includes paying for this damn wedding you don't want.

The words "simple" and "wedding" cannot belong in the same sentence around your fiancée.

The words "frivolous" and "wedding" always go in the same sentence, just not around your fiancée.

Weddings are showcases for the bride. You are just a cog in her grand scheme of things. Beware of this leading into the entire fiasco, and you may survive it okay.

Just make sure you won't have to pay to fly in her long lost relatives. This is a potential hidden expense most guys aren't warned about.

Why do napkins have to be so special in appearance? Mostly they are used by people who cannot stop drooling over the food or people crying from "how sweet" the whole thing is. Who really cares what the napkins look like?

Why spend a ton of money on table decorations that people get to take home? If you can't keep 'em, don't get 'em, I say.

Why is it that when picking out a dress, it has to be more expensive than your car?

I think the weeklong honeymoon to Fiji is cheaper than the dress that she will only wear one time.

With all the expenses you have, you'd better make sure you have no car payments, no student loans, no credit card debt, no outstanding loans or bills other than the bare minimum, or you'll be paying until you retire. Good luck.

Why is she allowed to pick everything she wants when registering for gifts, and you have no say? Aren't you supposed to be receiving these gifts too?

When obtaining rooms for the night of the wedding make sure her parents and your parents are in rooms at the opposite end of the hotel. That way noise will be allowed after all of the ceremonies (wink wink).

The best thing to do for the night of the wedding would be to book you and your new wife into a completely different hotel from everyone else so you don't get disturbed at all. What a pain.

Cocktail weenies, party subs, and Doritos are not acceptable appetizers at the reception.

Under no circumstances can burgers, fries, hot dogs, and pizza be served as the main course.

Everyone congratulates the bride, everyone consoles the groom, ever wonder why that is? It's because she was able to sucker a guy (YOU!) into a lifelong commitment to her.

You have to wait until that night or even later to consummate the marriage. You can't just up and leave after the minister says, "I now pronounce you husband and wife."

All the flowers and doves and foofiness around the whole day are enough to make any man sick.

You meet every single in-law, even the ones she didn't know she had.

You find out her long lost cousin is much hotter than she is and thinks you're hot too. TOO LATE, you're married now.

Did you ever notice that the beginning of "Here Comes the Bride" and the Death Song are the exact same notes just different pitches? Why do you think that is? I'll give you a hint, guys, they are both directed at you.

You actually have to get out in front of a bunch of people and dance! What's worse is your new bride says you aren't allowed to have any alcohol that day! How will you ever survive?!

You have to dance with the fat bridesmaids even though they are drunk and groping you.

You can't hang out with your friends, like usual you have to actually act like the people your parents made you invite are very important to you.

You must kiss her female relatives, some of the scariest women on the planet, on the cheek. They make Tammy Fae look natural.

You must hug her friends who are some of the ugliest women in the world.

It takes all you can muster to shake her father's hand and hug him after the wedding. This is the same man that has threatened to have you removed from the gene pool if you do anything at all wrong in the least.

You have to wear a tuxedo.

You have to act like the sex later that night isn't important to you while you are spending ten hours entertaining people you have never met before.

You have to eat an actual meal, like fish or chicken with vegetables, instead of the pizza and brats you wanted for the reception.

All that alcohol going around and you can't have a drop.

By the time the entire day is over, you are so exhausted, you fall asleep on the bed before your new bride comes out in the sexy negligee she bought for the occasion.

Your drunk friends become obnoxious, you think it's hysterical, she gets mad because they seem (to her) "to be ruining" the dance that night, and you don't get any.

Your ex-girlfriend shows up late, says an innocent congratulations, and your new bride gets jealous that she even showed up, another reason you aren't getting any that night.

The ENTIRE day must be absolutely perfect, no matter what, because it's her day.

You know that is impossible but need to play along if you want this marriage thing to work.

You must smile for hours at people you don't know.

The good part is that, most likely, you get to ride in a limo, but the bad part is you only have two blocks to go to the reception so a quickie is out of the question.

You have to be in everyone's picture.

You have to act like you enjoy being in thousands of pictures.

You have to meet all of her gorgeous female friends she hasn't let you meet until now. And you now know why, they are damn gorgeous and single.

If you are lucky enough to get married in Vegas or Atlantic City, she still won't let you gamble while you are there.

Make sure you don't plan the big day around any major sporting event, cause you know what will happen if you do--you won't get to see any of it.

You aren't allowed to remove the garter and look up her dress.

She puts your friends at the table in the corner so they won't distract anyone while they are getting drunk.

You have to wear a cumberbund.

You have to wear a bowtie.

You are not allowed to freeball in your tuxedo.

If you have a decent paying job, you will have to pay for the honeymoon. Don't expect that as a late wedding gift from any of her relatives.

All the gifts are addressed to her since she's the only one who will ever use them.

Be prepared to see kitchen appliances like never before when you open gifts.

You will see more worthless pieces of junk when you open your gifts than you could ever imagine.

Even though you wanted to just request money, she

said no, so now you get to write thank you letters for gifts, and you don't even know what they do.

You have to dance and have 300 people watch you at the reception.

Registering for wedding gifts at different stores does not ensure you will get the stuff you like.

Make sure to plan at least three days after you return from the honeymoon to go and return unwanted gifts.

Chapter 6

In-Laws

They stay at your house when they visit--this is very uncomfortable for men because the in-laws always take the room next to the master bedroom, making it impossible to partake in late night activities with your wife, especially those using the swing, whip, and handcuffs.

Her father is always suspicious of you--this was fine when you were only dating her as he had reason to be suspicious of you then. But after you've removed her from the dating pool he should express gratitude, not fear.

You can never do anything right in her parent's eyes – You are a computer tech guru for a multibillion dollar global corporation, making $100K+, but at any time you could get laid off. Then how would you support your family when your $500K portfolio runs out in six years?

You don't mow the lawn correctly--her father sits and watches you mow the lawn and tells you everything you are doing wrong, even though the lawn is evenly cut, and you are using a power mower.

You spend every evening and weekend playing with your kids, but her parents tell you that you spend too much time at your job.

You make enough money to support your family so your wife can stay home and raise your kids (something she wants to do until they are in school), but her parents think you are not supportive of her growing as a person.

You can't put your tools in the proper order, according to her dad.

You tie your tie wrong when getting ready for work.

Your facial hair (a neatly trimmed mustache) looks appalling and must go.

You don't force your kids to eat their vegetables, even though you make them have an apple for dessert.

Your kids need more discipline--yet they must do their homework first thing when they get home, and when they do something wrong they get punished appropriately for the infraction.

Your wife defends her parents' rude treatment of you saying they are just trying to protect her. The two of you get into a fight about it, and you end up sleeping on the couch for a week after telling her they are too possessive.

You fixed their twenty-five-year-old car, and it runs terrific. You'd just better make sure nothing happens to them in it EVER!

You went to Stanford, those damn Cardinals think they are so smart. Podunk University (PU), his alma mater, now that is the best damn school in the country!

Don't ever have a drink in front of her parents in the

first ten years of knowing them, otherwise you are a drunk and a potential alcoholic and could abuse her when you get out of control.

They say that the way her mother looks is the way your wife will look when she is that age. If her mom is butt ugly, you may want to reconsider, unless you aren't worried about twenty years down the road and are only worried about the present, then go for it and good luck.

How is it that according to her parents, you are the dumbest, worst man on the planet, yet your kids are the best, brightest, and sweetest kids on the planet? Especially since they are yours too!

You need to discipline your kids more and run the house like it is the army.

Your car, the safest minivan made, just isn't safe enough for her parents.

You drive like a maniac, even though you obey all traffic laws and follow at least three times the expected distance behind the car in front of you.

Your hair isn't combed right.

Don't cook dinner for them. No matter how pink the steaks are, they'll be overcooked.

Your barbeque isn't the right kind.

Your lawn mower doesn't do a good enough job.

That black shirt you have on is just the wrong shade of black.

Do you carry your money the way her father does? If not, you are carrying your money the wrong way.

Why would you ever by a house like this one in such a dangerous neighborhood? You get about one car an hour on the road in front of your house, but it's just not safe enough. What do they want, Fort Knox?

The gutters of your roof should be cleaned every two months according to her father. Yuck!

You are not allowed to carve the turkey for Thanksgiving dinner because her father is afraid you'll mangle the turkey, and there won't be any good pieces left.

You are not allowed to carve the ham for Christmas dinner simply because he wants to carve it.

Your kitchen knives are horrible for carving turkey or ham according to her father. Don't remind him that they are a wedding gift you received from him.

Your couch is too hard and not comfortable enough. Once you tell them their daughter picked it out, it's the best couch ever made.

The guest bed they are using isn't very comfortable, so you need to get a new mattress for them. Little do they know you planned it that way so they wouldn't stay more than a week.

You simply live too far away and must move closer. In other words, the house next door to them is finally for sale. If this ever happens, move across the country, unless they are there then of course you'd better stay where you are.

The swimming pool you put in the backyard isn't very safe for the kids. Of course you have a tarp for it and have a little security fence around it and cover it every night and drain it in the winter, but that just isn't sufficient.

Ever wonder why she never dated much in high school? Now you have met the reasons.

We haven't even begun to discuss her siblings and cousins, aunts and uncles.

If she comes from a large family (i.e., five kids or more) watch out. You will constantly be having the in-laws visiting, hopefully only for short periods of time (two days at most).

If one of her brothers played college football, be prepared to get slugged as a "love tap" every time you meet him, that is only if you pass his test and are a decent guy.

If her football playing brother doesn't like you... you're dead.

Of course we can't forget about her 250lb, 6'5" brother in the Navy Seals. He's always one of the wild ones first into battle. You are always safe, until you hurt his sister.

Then there's her sister, she marches to her own drummer. She has never worked a day in her life and still mooches off her parents at age forty. She says it enhances her creative abilities.

Lucky for you her sister likes to visit once a month for two weeks at a time.

We can't forget her eccentric aunt and uncle. They live on a boat in a small lake in Minnesota year-round. Just make sure you get a hotel whenever you go to visit them.

Her grandparents are another nightmare. They constantly bicker with each other and have gotten very good at it practicing over the last fifty-seven years.

After meeting her grandparents you are convinced their stubbornness in torturing each other is the only thing left keeping them alive. The worst part is you live in the same town, and she is their only nearby relative so you get to go keep them company all the time.

How can we forget her other sister and her five kids from hell?

The kids, ranging in age from three to eleven, have figured out how to destroy everything.

The worst part is your kids think their cousins are the

neatest kids on the planet and now want to mimic everything they see.

Whenever you visit her sister with the kids, you have to listen to her and her husband practicing to have more kids. At some point there should be a limit, and one of them should get fixed.

When visiting that sister, you and your wife get to sleep in the twins' room, and they have bunk beds.

Whatever you do, never, never, ever, ever go on a vacation with her parents.

Most likely her parents would want your first vacation with them to be YOUR honeymoon.

Chapter 7

Mood Swings (i.e., PMS)/Fights/ Arguments/Heated Discussions/Divorce

This reason can go in many categories, and you will probably see it in different forms. Women can be, and are, very illogical with no understandable reasons why they do the things they do. And you, as the man and supporter, need to come up with a logical answer to questions like, "Do these pants make me look fat and did the checkbook balance?" When multiple conflicting questions arise, it is better to act like you didn't hear her and were watching TV. In this type of scenario it is better to get in trouble for not listening then trying to navigate that kind of question land mine.

Women can cry at the drop of the hat for no reason, and they expect the same emotions from you. For example, you say, "Honey, I can't mow the lawn right now because it's raining." And whammo, she starts crying.

Women always need to talk about and share their feelings. Not only do they do this at the worst times (i.e., fourth quarter of the Super Bowl and it's a tie game), but they expect you to be willing to share your deepest and darkest secrets that only you and the stuffed teddy bear you had when you were four know about.

Will she be Dr. Jekyll or Mrs. Hyde tonight?

Question: Is it possible to say the right thing when it's "that time" of the month? Answer: NO!

You will never say the right thing. It was right yesterday, but she changed her mind five seconds ago, and you were supposed to know that, you ass.

How dare you not know that Bobby decided to drop Lana and started sleeping with Jessica in her favorite soap opera!!

You are having a wonderful conversation about your weekend plans when out of the blue she asks, "How many times have you done this with past girlfriends?" Forget it as you will never answer this correctly. You have the right to remain silent (although you will still be sleeping on the couch tonight), EVERYTHING you say can and WILL be held against you in a court of her. You have a right to get a friend on your side (although this will probably only make it worse), if you wish to waive these rights, kiss your ass goodbye and don't count on sex for at least a month. If you're lucky that is and she commutes your sentence down from six months.

She's hot and bothered as she walks out the door to go to work, so you make a nice romantic dinner reservation for two with a bottle of wine and get the hot tub ready at home. She calls you at lunch and says she is ready for you, you tell her you have a nice little surprise for her. She gets home, slams the door, and says she can never deal with her job again because she can't understand why they would change the filing system. No dinner, no wine, no hot tub, no fun for you, and how dare you think she would want that after the day she's had!

You cleaned the dishes right last time, are doing it the same way this time, but she wants it done differently now, how in the world could you not figure it out? Damn you anyway.

You are talking about what to do this weekend, haven't really discussed it yet at all, things are going well, then she erupts, "No way in hell are we going to the zoo this weekend!!!" Ouch, where did that come from? Don't even ask, just say, "I'm sorry, where would you like to go?" Probably won't work though.

You bring her flowers for no reason except that you care. You have never done anything wrong, all of a sudden she asks in a scream, "Who in the hell did you have sex with?" You definitely aren't getting any in the near future, no matter what you try. Just leave, let her read the sweet card, and hope she calls you back happy.

If she seems mad at something, and you try to listen, you may get lucky, and she'll be happy that you cared enough to listen. Just don't count on that reaction.

Sudden mood swings mean you don't have to do anything wrong, you will be sleeping on the couch anyway that night.

PMS is lethal for men simply because the woman knows or often times keeps track of when it's coming around. But she keeps it a secret from you, so you have to guess whether she is really mad or just has her hormones flying out of control to the point she's ready to rip your head off, and tomorrow she will be fine.

One time you will be allowed to wear your favorite shirt, the next time you try it's too grungy, and you can never wear it again. Try a month later, and she'll never remember that she nearly ripped it off of you because now it looks good again.

When moving into a house, be prepared to move the couch (by yourself) to at least ten different locations before she finds the location she likes. It always turns out to be the first place you put it.

Make the bed the way she taught you, and she will find something wrong with the way you made it, no matter what.

That picture on the wall of a mountain scene that's been in your family for generations looks great today; tomorrow, it is the ugliest thing she has ever seen.

The shoes she wore yesterday and felt so comfortable in, today are just the worst pair of shoes she's ever had in her entire life. Don't ask why or how; just agree with her, unless you don't mind sleeping on the couch.

How dare you say she's moody! She's never moody! She's always the sweetest person on the planet!

Black looked great on her last week. But now those same pants make her feel bloated and fat. Watch out if this happens. Refer to the clothing chapter on how to best handle these situations.

There are no way those kids could be hers, damn it. They are just too wild and they misbehave all the time. Funny, you could have sworn she was the one that gave birth to them, plus you are sure that both of you were there for the conception.

How in the world could you say that pain in the ass dog that she picked out is hers? It is so loud and unruly, it just has to be your dog, even though she is the one that is training it and spends tons of time with it.

She just can't eat any more. She has to stop cause she'll get too fat. Yeah, okay, she's 5'7" and weighs 115, like that would happen any time soon?

The kitchen is too small now. Granted she picked out that place because she liked the kitchen, but now she just has no room, so you are just going to have to move NOW.

Follow this simple rule when she is having one of those phases, and you may be able to survive: "DUCK!!"

If the previous doesn't work for you often, try this rule: Go for a nice, long, five-hour walk till she cools off.

Make sure the phrase "panties in a wad," isn't literal. If it is, offer to help and maybe you'll get lucky. If it's not literal then you are in trouble.

When it is "that time of the month," she will bite your head off one second and the next second not even know there was a problem. Whatever you do, don't ever bring up the reason she wanted to bite your head off in the first place, even if you are trying to resolve the issue, or you will be sleeping on the couch for the next several nights.

No matter what the truth is about anything, you can never be right if you ever want to have sex again.

In a divorce, they get half of the assets, but none of the debt. Now how fair is that?

Why is it that <u>you</u> always have to sleep on the couch?

You are always the one that has to move out when it's really heated and you are fighting about anything.

Don't be within throwing distance of your good china!

Make sure she cannot reach any sharp objects for at

least two days after a fight. Remember the Bobbitt story!

She is always right, even if she thinks that Tiger Woods is the best tennis player in the country, and Pete Sampras is the best figure skater she's ever seen. Don't bother with the hundreds of newspaper articles written daily about them. She's right if you ever want to sleep in your own bed again.

Have you ever had a woman apologize to you for being wrong about something? Know this--it will not happen. If it ever does, obtain a signed document by her and send it to me, cause otherwise I won't believe you.

Why is it she can get mad when you don't listen to her, but you can't get mad when she doesn't listen to you?

Many fights and such happen because men are unable to recognize the mood swings from above and so they try to be helpful, rather then just getting out of her way.

Just go sleep on the couch, expect it for at least a week.

If you have good news from work while you are banished to sleeping on the couch, even a 20 percent raise and a promotion, don't tell her. She will just get even more upset because you got a reward while she was mad at you.

I hope you have a good guest bed you can use. If you are lucky, she will allow you to sleep there instead of the couch.

Making up is not possible if you have offended her by saying something wrong about her parents, especially when they are visiting. She has to make it look good for them. Yes, it is a conspiracy.

If you ever want to go to a sporting event, you must take her. Wanting to go with a friend is a complete insult to her, at least in her eyes it is, even if it is his birthday, and he got the tickets for the two of you.

If you ever say the wrong thing about her clothes, even the tiniest little comment, you are in deep stuff. Refer to Chapter 4 for problems that can arise from these errors.

If you have to go through a divorce, remember this, you will not gain custody of the kids. Unless she has become an axe murderer and is in jail for life, then you have a chance. In other words, gaining custody of the kids won't happen.

You loved the dog right? Well, say goodbye, because just to spite you in the divorce, she's taking the dog, even though she can't stand it. There ain't nothing you can do about it.

In a divorce, you are screwed on general principles, because our society believes it is always the man's fault, and you don't deserve anything, even if she was having sex with every person under the sun. If you don't believe me just ask the judge. He thinks she's great in bed.

Don't expect to get your muscle car in the divorce either. She'll take the Camaro and three kids, and you'll get the minivan. She will do this just to spite you. Since the car is worthless to her, she will turn around and sell it for $1,000, then go out and buy a luxury SUV with her alimony payments.

Women have a tendency to throw things when you fight, so stay out of the dining room and away from the fine china or the knives in the kitchen.

Unfortunately when she starts getting angry, suggesting a mud pit and bikinis with some other women to burn off frustration will only get you slugged and won't be looked upon with good humor.

Chapter 8

Money

Your wife spends more money than you make, and you are the only one working. Where does that leave you? Filing for bankruptcy and divorce at the same time, cause she doesn't want you any more. And you are the only one stuck with the bad credit record and the debt to pay off since in a divorce, the wife gets half the assets and none of the debt. What a rip off for guys. Who needs this kind of hassle and garbage to go through anyway?

As my mom always says, "What's mine is mine and what's his is ours." At least she's polite when she jokes about it. Think of all the women out there that are serious about that.

Most women think, "What's mine is mine and what's his is mine." Either way, you get screwed.

You can't get the chainsaw you need to get rid of the dead trees in the backyard, which she's been complaining about for months, until she gets that gorgeous pink dress in the Nordstrom's catalog she's been eyeing for months, even though she has no clue when she will ever wear it. Makes perfect monetary sense, doesn't it?

When buying a house, it must have a washer and dryer for clothes (the Laundromat a block away just isn't convenient enough), a garbage disposal (trash cans can't hold trash anymore they have to be used for recyclables), and a dishwasher (actually, you should request that, otherwise scrubbing dishes will be a nightly chore for you), but a workbench and work area is out of the question. Right, who needs to have a place for tools for common housework needs anyway?

Women do not know the meaning of the phrase, "Balancing a checkbook."

Be prepared to start setting money aside for trips for two, instead of one.

Be prepared to need to put additional money into the car, because the car she drives will not get the oil changed frequently enough, and it will have engine troubles.

If you want to get anything for yourself that costs over $20 you have to beg for it for days, and most likely even weeks, on end.

She will spend $50 on her like it's nothing and won't think twice about it.

You can't complain about her spending $50 on her, no matter what. It's not an option or even a possible topic of discussion if you ever want sex again and ever want to get anything for yourself at any price.

If you want a new lawn mower, because it would cost $300 to fix the old one, be prepared to give a chart presentation on the benefits of a new lawn mower.

If she blows up the car, when you do finally get a new car for the family you get the old one. She automatically gets the new one; it's some sort of right of passage.

You can't pick a car you like since you will never drive it. You have to pick one you would never drive and pretend it's the best car on the planet. No matter that buying a new car is expensive these days cause car manufacturers can't make a car and sell it for under $20K, more than half your annual salary.

Shopping and spending money are to women as watching sports and a love of cars are to men.

Ads are designed to exploit a woman's inability to understand value, like that damn Volkswagen beetle with a list price of $22K. It's a glorified sardine can, but women love it. Make sure if you are buying a car, you don't go anywhere near a Volkswagen dealership just for that reason.

When a woman goes to buy shoes (oh, no, the sacred topic!!!), she can never buy just one pair. She can break the bank even if she shops at Payless because she will find this pair for this outfit and that pair for that outfit and a third pair for another outfit and a fourth pair for a fourth outfit. It just keeps going and going.

Women must keep up with the in crowd and that means buying the "right" everything. The worst part is that fashion magazines change this every season--spring, summer, fall and winter.

They've even made holidays seasons of their own specifically to exploit a woman's need to constantly be in season like Valentine's Day, St. Patrick's Day, Easter, Summer, Labor Day, Halloween, before Thanksgiving, Christmas, etc. Each season is now designed to have women wanting to buy more stuff to show off their holiday/season spirit.

Women need to have at least forty or fifty fashion

magazine subscriptions to keep up with all the changes, at $30 per subscription, you figure it out. Ouch, there goes your season tickets to the baseball team.

Banking is a foreign concept to women. They think as long as there are still checks in the checkbook, they must have money to spend.

To women, money grows on trees. It only does in an artificial sense though since dollar bills are made of paper, and paper comes from trees. You can't pick it from trees like apples. It doesn't fall from the sky like babies do from the stork.

You will never get to have the checkbook in your possession unless it is the weekend and you ask for it to buy her something she wants or needs, like feminine products.

Look in the Clothes chapter to understand shopping and clothing spending habits.

Makeup is extremely expensive, and she has to have thirty shades of blush and eye shadow to match all of her clothes.

Nail polish is another thing women can't seem to have enough of. Those 200 bottles, each a different shade, take a small collection of paychecks to afford as well.

Women also spend a small fortune on hair care products, including hair spray, straightening spray, curling spray, shampoo, conditioner, coloring, curling irons, hair dryers, etc. It's amazing there is any room in the bathroom for your stuff. All of this is what keeps small countries' economies growing.

The big question is whether to pay bills or allow her to go on another shopping spree. Guess who wins and why you still have bills and fight about it all the time.

There is always a need to have an extra set of dishes for no special occasion. For men who don't know, dishes are expensive. This should not be an impulse buy though women will often treat it like one.

Women also feel a need to have four or five sets of glasses in the kitchen. For men who don't know, this can also get very expensive. Take it from a bachelor who has purchased one set of his own.

A woman will always say they absolutely have to have something, even if they don't know what it is or when they would use it. At that point in time, it's as good as purchased.

A nice restaurant to a guy is a clean sports bar. A nice restaurant to a woman is $25-$35 per entrée. There is a huge difference here in price and preferences.

Money is the root of all evils. It also pays the bills so where does that leave you?

Perceptions about worth are a huge issue between men and women. Men see value in lawn and car tools. Women see value in home furnishings and home ambiance. This leads to numerous quarrels on where to spend money. Count on you losing.

You have to start saving for your child's college education the minute the child is conceived if you have any hopes of being able to afford it someday.

For each child you have, expect school to cost approximately 10 percent more for each two years difference in age. So if you have four kids, each two years apart, the fourth kid will cost over 30 percent more for college than the first kid. Ugly numbers considering a four-year college now costs about $60K. In ten years that will close in on $80K, if not surpass it.

So college for one child in ten years will cost the same, and possibly more, as that sweet Corvette convertible you've been eyeing since you turned twenty.

If you try to keep expenses separate as a couple, be prepared for all of your money to go to the kids and savings, while all her money goes to her extravagant shopping needs.

If you keep expenses separate, she will insist on seeing how much you have in your accounts and how you spend it, but you won't have any access to her money or any idea of what she does with it.

If expenses are separate, you will be expected to pay for any date the two of you go on, even if you are married.

How is it possible that you are only "allowed" to have $20 in your wallet at a time, but she gets the checkbook and credit cards and must have hundreds in cash "for emergencies"?

Kitchen appliances are very expensive, and of course she will insist on all the best ones for "her" kitchen. Can you believe a coffee maker can be over $100?

She will also insist on having the finest sheets for the bed, plus she'll need four sets for emergencies. Decent sheets are $150 including fitted sheet, top sheet, and two pillowcases. Very good sheets are $250, but the finest are more expensive than new desktop computers. How does that seem right since you aren't even conscious 95percent+ of the time you use sheets?

Women accessorize, and accessorizing as they do costs money. Believe it or not, $200 cell phones are now considered a necessary accessory instead of a $40 phone that still does the job.

Fine jewelry does not consist of cubic zirconium. Damn, especially since it looks pretty good, and you can get it for less than a burger at McDonald's.

Picture money going down the drain with the following scenario. She wants a cat, so you get a cat. She won't let you declaw the cat, and then she decides she wants a leather sofa and chair. Enough said.

She has a very unique, and what turns out to be extremely expensive, hobby of fine china collecting.

She also likes to collect pottery from local artists. Believe it or not, a dinner size plate can cost $100. Just think how much a collection of a hundred pieces of varying shapes and sizes will cost.

Your hobby of collecting baseball cards just isn't a very wise investment, however you have a mint condition Mickey Mantle rookie card passed down to you over the years that is worth more than her pottery collection. If you tell her that she'll hock it for more pots.

You can't have a hobby that requires money, unless it includes yard work or cleaning the house gutters, because that would mean less for her to spend.

Can you believe she wants a $2,000 mountain bike that she will ride once or twice a year at most? Ugh!

She wants to buy a pair of $500 snow skies, but she has never skied before in her life. What if she hates it? Too bad, she's decided she has to have a pair just in case she likes it.

Of course if you want a pair of snow skies you have to go and rent a pair first, just in case you don't like to ski, then you won't waste money, but it's okay for her.

Chapter 9

Kids, Family Life and Having
a Midlife Crisis with a Family

If you have a daughter--dating--need I say more? Okay, I will. Go and get yourself a shotgun and a sign next to the case saying "Animals are only for practice."

You need to have a year supply of band-aids on hand if you have any sons. However, that supply will really only last about a week.

As teenagers, they can eat more in a day then an entire football team for a pre-game meal.

You'd better have great health insurance with sons. And that just seems to get harder and harder to find every day with our health care system. Good luck.

The kids are always yours when they do something wrong. This automatically makes you the mean, bad parent cause you have to give out the punishment.

You must keep things out of the reach of your kids that you wouldn't otherwise have to worry about, like your stash of Playboys.

You have to explain "Why?" for everything. Kids can't accept an answer because you say so. It just takes so long and they always seem to want to know "Why?" in the last two minutes of the football game with your team down by two and driving.

You have to change diapers. With and without poop, with and without pee, doesn't matter, you still have to change diapers.

After changing a diaper, especially after a mess, you have to put your hands very close to all that mess to wipe them clean.

How can babies throw up so much? They hardly eat anything.

Sleeping with a newborn is impossible. At least she's the one that has to get up to breastfeed.

Just remember, for every time she has to get up for the baby at night, she'll remind you of it for years to come. A waking baby will haunt you after it has gone through college and graduated.

You have to pay for college or at least make it look like you will pay for college.

Hosing off the baby with the garden hose is not an acceptable option for giving them a bath. At least not until they turn two, and then it becomes inevitable.

You cannot let your Great Dane lick the baby clean after meals.

After making the baby, the fun is over.

You must prepare for your pregnant wife the most insane and disgusting meals never heard of. There is a reason you have never heard of a tuna, garlic, pickle, and ice cream shake before now.

Have you ever smelled such disgusting odors from such a little thing? Not even Al Bundy's feet are that raunchy.

You will be called every name in the book, and even names you haven't heard of, during the birth of your child.

Your computer den is now the baby's room, but her sewing room is still intact.

Kids will try anything. Even things they aren't supposed to, like seeing if they can fly by hanging on the ceiling fan.

You are the one that has to give the talk about sex. Your wife will teach the daughter about female issues, but not about sex.

In order to teach the daughter about sex, it is not

enough to say that she can't have any until she is twenty-five and married, you have to go buy a $200 shotgun to help enforce it.

You have to teach kids that alcohol is bad, even though you like to have a few beers every day after work.

Drugs are a major concern. You have to now deal with the fact that kids have easier access to drugs then you ever did.

Sexually transmitted diseases are a major concern too. Telling them to slap on a condom isn't enough any more.

Topics like those are hard, because your parents never told you a thing about any of it, so now you have to make up the speech as you go. You suck at giving speeches.

You have to continually reinforce that fact that even though cats do land on their feet, they should not test this theory on your cat from the second floor deck. (My brother and I tried it once to our cat, and it worked. She still lived another ten plus years! I don't recommend it though.)

While playing doctor for kids can be fun, make sure they have no clue what an enema of any kind is. The results could be very messy, in more ways then one.

Twister is a great game for kids to play, just make sure they don't see you and your wife playing naked twister, or they will really be in for it when they suggest that game at a friend's house.

Kids will copy what you do. If you scratch, they will scratch, if you burp, they will burp, if you fart, they will fart, and they won't realize these are things that shouldn't be done in public. Be ready to be embarrassed in public by these actions more then once.

Sooner or later your son will beat you at hoops. Once that happens be prepared to not live it down for years to come.

Sooner or later your daughter will beat you at hoops. Once that happens you will never be able to live that down because your wife will always give you hell about it.

Unfortunately, after about sixteen years dealing with your kids, the inevitable will happen. They will learn how to drive.

This is impossible to avoid unless you pack up and move to Fiji, something that probably wouldn't go over very well with your wife.

Patience is a virtue you will need from birth till you can kick them out at eighteen, and even then it won't end.

If you thought you had patience before, wait till you have kids.

It is very possible you will become great friends with your kids' pediatrician. Your wallet will become your pediatrician's best friend.

Once your kids can drive, your insurance agent will be your best friend and not for the reasons you'd like.

Once your kids can drive, the used car dealer will become another best friend.

Getting a nice little sports car, like a Corvette convertible, and putting kids in the back, doesn't quite feel the same.

That 65" screen TV you've been wanting for years doesn't fit in the family room.

If the 65" screen TV does fit, you never get to watch anything on it you want, especially sports. She watches soaps and Fried Green Tomatoes on it all the time.

Changing jobs to become a great chef is impossible since you pay all the bills so she can stay home and raise the kids. You have to stick out the same old job, at least until the kids finish college.

You can't binge on pie, cake, and ice cream because that was your daily routine. She still makes you drink lite beer and eat healthy. Hey, just be glad you still get to drink beer.

Staying out all night checking out the nightlife is not an option, no matter what.

Wearing extra gold around your neck trying to relive your youth doesn't have the same fervor.

You can't go buy expensive clothing for yourself to look good, the kids will get mad and jealous, the wife will get suspicious and stop you from going out, EVER!

Getting a muscle car means souping up the minivan.

Flirting with a younger woman means you'd be hitting on your son's dates, may not be a bad thing if it works, but I doubt your wife or son would be happy with you.

A hot night out means taking the family to the Indian restaurant in town for really spicy food.

A hot date means getting a babysitter for the night so you can go out with your wife of twenty years who's looking a lot like her mom. Is that good or bad? You have to decide that one.

If you start working out for the first time in your marriage, your wife will wonder why and wonder who you are trying to impress cause it sure as hell wouldn't be her.

If you are showing any signs of going through a midlife crisis, do not, I repeat, DO NOT, ever say you have to spend a late night at the office, especially if that is something you don't usually do. Your wife will track you down expecting that you are having an affair.

Don't go buy a tank top for going to the swimming pool or beach if that is something you hadn't done before. Your wife will wonder who you are trying to show off for. We both know it's the beach babes, but she will get mad.

If you all of a sudden decide to change the type of underwear you wear, you will be quizzed worse than the people on "Who Wants to Be a Millionaire."

If you want to change your hairstyle, you will again be quizzed unmercifully as to why. The answer, "I just wanted a change of pace," won't pass the wife test either.

If you bike on a regular basis, don't go buy bike shorts. Once again the unmerciful barrage of questions will hit you.

Jogging renders similar problems. You can't all of a sudden start going without a shirt, she'll think you run by "hot babes" all the time and are trying to get their attention.

Dyeing your hair is cause for suspicion rather than just for your own peace of mind.

Going on a diet to change yourself is also cause for suspicion rather than wanting to feel healthy and young again.

Getting a hot car means getting a four-door sedan rather than a minivan.

It's tough to spend money on toys for yourself when the kids always want new bikes, new clothes, new $200 shoes, etc.

Changing careers is nearly impossible, especially if your job of choice includes flipping burgers at Hooters.

Becoming a bouncer at a nightclub may have been a good choice when you were twenty and single, but the wife definitely won't let that happen now at forty.

Wanting to become a bartender would have the same results as wanting to become a bouncer.

If you are the only breadwinner of the house, changing careers to something that pays $10/hr because it's what you've always wanted to do when your family has been used to you making $50/hr is impossible.

Skydiving, unless you are certified, will most likely not be allowed by your wife.

Bungee jumping, unless you are certified, will most likely not be allowed by your wife.

Hang gliding, unless you are certified, will most likely not be allowed by your wife.

Rock climbing, unless you are certified, will most likely not be allowed by your wife.

If you are lucky you might get away with parasailing.

Unless you have been doing it for years, suddenly meeting the guys in Vegas for a long weekend probably would not go over well with your wife, especially if she doesn't go with you.

Camping weekends with the guys may be difficult to pass off as well, refer to the Chapter on Mood Swings, etc., for problems here.

Doing just about anything with the guys all of a sudden could be difficult, unless you've set precedence over the years.

Moving into a large studio apartment with a family of four because it's a more open place is simply not possible.

Getting a motorcycle will most likely not be allowed,

especially if you want to buy all the leather clothes to go with it.

Getting a boat will most likely mean getting a pontoon boat, rather than a speedboat, the obvious choice for most guys.

Buying almost anything significant is nearly impossible because you are still expected to put the kids through college.

Chapter 10

Unclassifiable, Still Undeniable

Whenever a guy (maybe a couple of guys) is with a group of women, just to make the man (or men) feel uncomfortable, the women bring feminine products into the discussion. The potential of being stuck in this situation increases dramatically with marriage.

Whenever you decide to get into a car with a female driver and other females, it is a good idea to know for sure that your health insurance is current.

Women discuss men's butts as if it was an accessory rather than a body part, yet women insist men are more crass then women. Yeah, we stare at their breasts, but that's because we don't have our own, they have their own butts!

Her friends, no matter how obnoxious, are okay to hang around, but your best friend from the last twenty years is a jackass if he ever does one little thing wrong.

If she doesn't like your friend, be prepared to go to his wedding alone, because she is too stubborn to go. However, if her friend is the obnoxious one, you WILL go to her wedding, no matter how painful, kicking and screaming, if you ever want to sleep in your own bed again.

You are not allowed to get your way for anything, **<u>EVER!!!!!</u>** It's not acceptable in the female's "code of conduct." Why is this you ask? Because women know men will cave in with time, no matter how wrong the woman is, just to get back in their own bed and end the fighting.

If you love animals, they hate them. If you hate animals, they love them. It's just to make sure they like the exact opposite things you do.

Women are just too temperamental to ever try to figure out. If you try they will change the rules. It's not fair but they do it anyway.

When getting a babysitter, you must select one that is only about twelve or thirteen and very ugly. Trust me, don't ask why, just do it.

When grocery shopping, the usual TV dinners will not be purchased any more.

You have to get used to home cooking. Pray you find a wife that knows how to cook and doesn't burn the JELLO.

When selecting a pet, if you hate cats, she will want a cat.

When selecting a pet, if you hate dogs, she will get a dog.

When selecting a pet, if you hate birds, she will get a bird.

When selecting a pet, if you hate fish, she will get a 50 gallon aquarium and fill it with fish.

When trying to get dressed for work, if you're late, she will want to have sex. Then when you try to have sex when you get back from work, she will turn you down.

When you get home from work horny because you thought about her trying to get you that morning, she will have a headache and won't even touch you.

When you want seafood for dinner, she will need Thai food.

When you want Chinese food for dinner, she will need Italian.

What do the past seven reasons have in common? No matter what you want, she will say she wants something different, even if she actually wants the same thing you do.

If she laughs in bed, just make sure her head wasn't under the covers first.

Men Beware: With today's lifestyles and everything so open, RuPaul is becoming the standard, so the she could actually be a he. Do a package check, especially in unique or wild clubs.

Women are allowed to change their minds and opinions at the drop of a dime, yet men aren't allowed to change their opinions at all.

Men are only allowed, in fact more accurately demanded, to change their personality, but everything else has to stay the same.

Even if you are telling the truth--it could be about anything at all--a typical woman's response will be to not believe you.

Women typically don't know basic car maintenance like checking the oil, keeping the car filled with gas, getting it serviced regularly, etc. So a very nice car in her possession could become a piece of junk before the loan is paid off.

Women are not good with hooking up electronics.

Make sure she stays away from all of the cables and wires in the entertainment center otherwise it will take you months to fix her mess.

Keep women away from the project if you add on to your home. This can only be disaster if she tries to help build it, unless she's a carpenter, then you're in luck.

Why is it that the car radio must always be set to the station she likes?

No sports talk radio in the car when she's around.

Most likely you will get stuck listening to easy listening music in the car.

If you don't get stuck listening to easy listening music, you'll get stuck listening to marriage and relationship counseling radio shows.

No matter how much you try to explain it to them, women will never be able to understand men's obsessions with motor vehicles (i.e., motorcycles and sports cars).

Why is it that the wife always has a nice room in the house for herself, such as a sewing room, but men are always relegated to the garage and the shed?

Only challenge a woman to a sport if you know you can put her in her place at any time. If she can beat you at will, you will never live it down from her, and she will always rub it in.

When being a gentleman it is nearly impossible to get both doors at a restaurant without being awkward. This is a skill men still need to perfect since sometimes women expect it.

Some women get upset if a man opens a door for them, so you have to learn in the first thirty seconds if she wants doors opened for her, or if she's a women's libber so as not to upset her either way.

If women want equal rights, shouldn't they also be willing to open doors for us without making comments like "I can't believe you are making me open the door" when we would have had to run to get to the door first?

Why is it okay for a woman to make sexual innuendos, but if you do it you are either a sexist or horny?

Why is it women have to put on their makeup while driving the car? Isn't driving dangerous enough without people ignoring the road because they are preoccupied with their eyeliner?

Can you believe there is an adapter for women to plug in their hair dryers while driving? Can the roads get any more dangerous?

Of course the roads can more dangerous, give the women their hair dryers while they are texting their friends about a lunch date while they are driving.

Once women are able to blow dry their hair in the car, you know it's only a matter of time before one of them decides to curl their hair while driving too.

A man must make sure the woman never drives, just in case she decides she must do one of the "maintenance" tasks mentioned above. That typically will lead to fighting, and we all know what happens then.

Men can get packed for a weeklong trip in about forty-five minutes, give or take three minutes. Once a woman becomes involved it's a weeklong ordeal just to pack. Even if you are going to a beach resort, and the only thing you'll need is a bathing suit.

Here are 12 reasons men prefer pizza over women:

A pizza is easier to pick up.

A pizza accepts you the way you are.

With a pizza there is no risk of social diseases.

A pizza is ready when you are.

Satisfaction guaranteed when you order a pizza.

You always get exactly what you want and nothing you don't with a pizza.

You can't be accused of sexual harassment if you drool over the pizza.

A pizza doesn't say no.

A pizza won't complain if you want to have a beer with it.

You can order two pizzas, and neither will get jealous of the other one.

With a pizza, you always get quick delivery.

With a pizza, there is no role confusion.

Breinigsville, PA USA
05 December 2010
250701BV00001B/1/P